Worship Is... What?!

Rethinking Our Ideas About Worship

TOM KRAEUTER

Emerald Books

P.O. BOX 635
Lynnwood, WA 98036

Training Resources
Hillsboro, Missouri

Emerald Books are distributed through YWAM Publishing. For a full list of titles, including other great worship resources, visit our website at www.ywampublishing.com or call 1-800-922-2143.

Worship Is...What?!

Copyright © 1996 by Training Resources
                        8929 Old LeMay Ferry Road
                        Hillsboro, MO 63050
                        (636) 789-4522
                        www.training-resources.org

10 09 08 07 06 05 04   10 9 8 7 6 5 4

Published by Emerald Books
P.O. Box 635
Lynnwood, Washington 98046

ISBN 1-883002-38-9

All Scripture quotations are from either the King James Version or The Holy Bible, New International Version, copyright © 1973, 1978, 1984 International Bible Society. Used by permission of Zondervan Bible Publishers.

Printed in the United States of America.

Dedication

I humbly dedicate this book to my wonderful wife, Barbara. For nearly 18 years of marriage (and a few years prior to) you have loved me in ways beyond my understanding. You have accepted me with all of my quirks and foibles. From your love I have learned much about God's love for me and how to love others. You're the best! Thanks!

Other books by Tom Kraeuter

Thanks...

...to those who reviewed the unedited manuscript and offered thoughts to make it stronger: Pastor Les and Barbara Youn of Living Word Fellowship, Voluntown, Connecticut, and Pastor Bill Koster of Faith Reformed Church, Portage, Michigan.

...to those whose writings and teachings have been a major inspiration in my life and ministry, most notably Pastor Nick Ittzes, Dr. Judson Cornwall, R.C. Sproul and Dr. Robert Webber.

...to Jennifer Brody who once again did a magnificent job of making my writing acceptable for publication.

...to my children, David, Stephen and Amy, for allowing me the time to make this book a reality.

Table of Contents

Forward

Some time ago, my good friend Chuck Fromm, the CEO of Maranatha! Music, gave me a one-liner that I have quoted to many people:

"Let's face it, Bob, twenty years ago when a person moved to town they asked, 'Where's the best preaching?' Today, when they move to a new place they ask, 'Where's the best worship?'"

Twenty years ago, most Protestant churches were not even interested in discussing the issue of worship; almost no books existed on the subject; conferences on the topic were nearly non-existent. The subject was relegated to the farthest back burner of issues facing the church.

Now, all of that has changed. Drastically. A seismic shift has occurred from no interest to a primary interest in worship. There is a plethora of new books, a multitude of conferences, and an entire industry based on the worship phenomena.

Yet, worship is barely understood, let alone practiced well in the local church.

Into this arena comes this forthright book by Tom Kraeuter, *Worship Is...What?!*

In simple yet profound terms, Tom Kraeuter gives us a popular insight into the most profound details of the worship experience.

It is the priority of our life.

It must start in the heart.

It proceeds from the heart to action.

It is a *response* to God, a giving to God.

So, we ask, what happens when we worship:

The *conscience* is quickened by the holiness of God;

The *mind* is fed by the word of God

The *heart* is open to the love of God

The *will* is devoted to the purpose of God

Consequently, worship becomes

A way of life;
A doing to others;
A life spent with God.

Tom Kraeuter's words are to the point. You don't have to try to figure out what he is saying. He speaks to the issue of worship and of the matter of true worship.
Take up the book and read.
And then do it as he says it.
It's on the mark.

Robert Webber
Professor of Theology, Wheaton College
Editor: *The Complete Library of Christian Worship*

Introduction

Most people do not read long book introductions. If I promise to be brief will you read it?

Not long ago John Piper, pastor of Bethlehem Baptist Church in Minneapolis, Minnesota, was one of the main speakers at a conference. He made a statement that in some ways revolutionized my thinking on worship. Although I failed to copy the statement verbatim (shorthand has never been one of my strong points) this is the basic gist of what he said: "There are two great passions in the universe: God's passion to be glorified and man's passion to be satisfied. However, these two do not need to conflict. They can come to simultaneous fulfillment through worship, because God is most glorified in me when I am most satisfied in Him alone."

It's true. There is something fulfilling about worship. Unfortunately it is not fulfilling for everyone. I am increasingly convinced that this, at least in part, is due to our lack of true understanding of biblical worship.

Most people formulate their ideas about worship more from experience, both their own and others', than from a truly scriptural perspective. I know this is true for my life also. Many of the ideas I have had regarding worship came from experiences in church as a child. These are not necessarily all bad, but they are not necessarily all biblical either. At least part of the reason that this happens is because the Bible never directly defines worship. In order to truly grasp the concept one must really dig.

Because the Scriptures do not give us a specific definition of worship, I thought it would be good to offer some thoughts to help us understand this broad topic. Through the years I have encountered numerous definitions of worship. None have, from my study of true biblical worship, been adequate definitions in and of themselves. Some have fallen far short of the mark. Others have offered some profound insights into the real nature of worship.

In this book I would like to share some of these various definitions, some in part, some complete. Each will be expounded upon to make them practical and helpful for people in our society and culture.

My hope and prayer is that your idea of worship and how it applies to your life will be stretched and expanded to come closer to the fullness of God's desire for you as His child.

Worship: *The* Priority

Definition: Worship is our reason for being.

One of the most common questions that has disturbed the mind of mankind throughout history is this: why are we here; what is our purpose? People of every generation have pondered this question. Fortunately, Scripture clearly depicts the reason for our existence: to worship God.

When we begin to understand that worship is our reason for being, it will revolutionize our thinking in every area of life. However, the concept of worship can mean different things to different people. To some, this word brings to mind reflective moments sensing the reality of the presence of God. For others it can mean any one of various physical expressions (lifting hands, kneeling, dancing, etc.) of adoration to their Savior. Still others find the height of worship in learning new truths from the Word of God. All of these, and numerous other expressions, can be worship.

Unfortunately, to many people today the idea of praise and worship brings to mind simply a current fad, something that will soon pass. They think of certain musical styles or instrumentation that are trendy but not enduring; a "now" sound that will soon fade in popularity. However, praise and worship is much more than a current fad.

It is very clear from Scripture and other sources that our main purpose in life is to worship God. Although this is never directly stated in Scripture, it is obvious from the consistent references made to the importance of worship that the real reason the Lord made us was to worship Him.

One of the best places to readily make this observation is in the original ten commandments God gave His people. The first three commandments all deal with our worshipping God only. First He tells us to have no other gods before Him; second He instructs us to have no idols, and third He commands that we not misuse His name (Exodus 20:2-7).

Think for a moment about the implications of giving the people ten commandments set in stone. If you had the opportunity to start a brand-new country and could give the people just ten laws by which to run the nation, what would you deem most important? Would you "waste" three of your laws in an effort to impress upon the people that worshipping God is first priority? The Lord obviously thought it was that important. The first three of the original ten rules had worship as their focus.

This focus is even reflected in the way God had the Israelites set up their camp in the desert. He commanded that three tribes be positioned to the north, three to the south, three to the east and three to the west. At the very center of the camp God commanded that they set up the tabernacle containing the Ark of the Covenant and the Holy of Holies.

Why did God make this kind of arrangement for their camp? God was communicating a spiritual principle via this physical encampment. The spiritual principle was that no matter what they were doing — from finding new ways to cook manna to getting married, transacting business or having sex — God wanted them to know that the very center of their lives was worship. Life in the nation of Israel was to evolve around the worship of God [Nathan, Rich and Wilson, Ken, *Empowered Evangelicals*, (Ann Arbor, Vine Books, 1995), pp. 154-155].

Peter's first letter offers a very clear understanding

of our purpose. Peter tells us that unbelievers "stumble because they disobey the message" (1 Peter 2:8b). He then goes on to contrast this with the lives of believers. "But you are a chosen people, a royal priesthood, a holy nation, a people belonging to God..." (1 Peter 2:9a). Peter continues this sentence with what grammatically is referred to as a purpose clause, "...that you may..." The words following a purpose clause give the purpose or reason for what was stated previously. He tells us that the reason we are a chosen people, a royal priesthood and a holy nation is so that we may "declare the praises of Him who called you out of darkness into His wonderful light" (1 Peter 2:9b). Our reason for being is to declare His praises.

Throughout John's Revelation we see glimpses of heaven. In each of those heavenly snapshots the main activity is worship. Throughout eternity what we will be involved in is not evangelistic crusades, not teaching Sunday School classes. We will not be witnessing to our neighbors or engaging in spiritual warfare. Our main activity in heaven will be worship.

In the fourth chapter of Revelation, John relates seeing the throne of God and the thrones of the twenty-four elders surrounding it. He mentions the awesomeness of God's presence ("flashes of lightning, rumblings and peals of thunder"). In great detail he describes the "four living creatures" that were near the throne. He then tells their function. "Day and night they never stop saying: 'Holy, holy, holy is the Lord God Almighty, who was, and is, and is to come.'" Then John goes on to describe the activity of the entire scene he has just painted for us. "Whenever the living creatures give glory, honor and thanks to Him who sits on the throne and who lives for ever and ever, the twenty-four elders fall down before Him who sits on the throne, and worship him who lives for ever and ever. They lay their crowns before the throne and say: 'You are worthy, our Lord and God, to receive glory and honor and power, for You created all things, and by Your will they were created and have their being'" (Revelation 4:2-11). Worship.

Not only does John depict worship as the main activity of those whose natural habitat is heaven, he also clearly portrays it as the chief function of those who previously lived on earth. In Revelation 15 he describes the "sea of glass mixed with fire." Standing beside the sea were the saints of God "who had been victorious over the beast and his image and over the number of his name." John goes on to again portray the activity of the scene.

> They held harps given them by God and sang the song of Moses the servant of God and the song of the Lamb: "Great and marvelous are Your deeds, Lord God Almighty. Just and true are Your ways, King of the ages. Who will not fear You, O Lord, and bring glory to Your name? For You alone are holy. All nations will come and worship before You, for Your righteous acts have been revealed" (Revelation 15:2-4).

Again, worship. Wholehearted, unashamed, unabashed worship.

We can often catch a glimpse of someone's true feelings about a certain topic from their emotional reactions. Recently I began looking at the times in Scripture when God became angry. It is interesting to note that nearly every time the Lord expressed His wrath toward His own people it was because of one of two reasons: either they were directly involved in idolatry or they were trusting in themselves for provision instead of God. In either case the reality is that they were refusing to give God the honor, or worship, of which only He is worthy. And because of this He showed His rage.

Please understand that God is certainly not insecure. He is not throwing a childish temper tantrum. His anger is forthcoming because His people consistently violate the reason for which He created them — worship. Throughout the Scriptures the Lord demonstrates the priority of worship by His reaction to non-worship and false worship.

When the Lord told Pharaoh of Egypt to let the people of Israel go free, His reason was simple: that they might worship God. The very reason He created man is put forth to Pharaoh as the emphatic reason for allowing the Israelites to leave: to worship their Creator.

In the sixth chapter of Matthew, Jesus was teaching His disciples to pray using what we commonly refer to as the Lord's Prayer. Do you recall the opening words? "Our Father in heaven, hallowed be Your name..." This is not a statement of fact. If it were Jesus would have said, "Your name *is* hallowed." Instead, the Greek seems to be a bit unclear; it is either a petition ("Father, let Your name be revered by men as holy") or a statement of worship ("Father, we honor Your name as holy..."). In either case the final scenario is worship.

The writers of the *Westminster Catechism* put it this way: "The chief end of man is to glorify God and enjoy Him forever." Without question our reason for existing is to worship God.

Charles Stanley, in his tape series *Worship: A Biblical View*, asks, "Is there anything that God needs? Is there anything He cannot provide for Himself? 'No' to both questions. Can you name the thing that God wants from us above anything else? He wants us to worship Him, motivated by love and devotion to Him because of Who He is."

> Worship is written upon the heart of man by the hand of God... In a broad sense worship is inseparable from and is an expression of life. It is not that man cannot live without worship, it is that he cannot truly live without worship... man was made to worship as surely as he was made to breathe. We may restrict the expression of worship for a season, just as we may briefly hold our breath, but there is an inward craving for worship that cannot be permanently stilled [Judson Cornwall, quoted by Don McMinn in *The Practice of Praise*, (Waco, Word, 1992)].

The last thing Satan tempted Jesus with in the desert was for Jesus to worship him (Matthew 4:9). Even the enemy of our souls understands the priority of worship. The truth is that Satan will often tempt you and me in the same way he did Jesus. And if he cannot get us to worship him then he will do everything he can to keep us from worshipping God. He will try to keep us busy with mundane tasks, problems in life, etc. He will even help keep us busy with church activities in order to keep us from focusing on the Lord and worshipping Him. Do not fall for his ploys.

Worship. It is and always will be our first priority.

Worship: Heart *and* Action

Definition: Worship is wholehearted, passionate adoration of our Creator/Redeemer

Okay, so now that we understand that worship is truly our reason for existence, *what is it*? Well, to start with, true Biblical worship is not passive. Almost by definition worship involves action on our part.

When I was in seminary, one of the professors gave us an assignment. We were to do a word study on the word "worship." We were required to use all available resources to research the literal renderings of the word "worship." We were expected to search out what the various Hebrew and Greek words that we translate "worship" really mean and report our findings to the class.

Although the assignment required a great deal of work I was eager to dig in. I made preparations for the assignment. I had stacks of reference books to assist me (this was before computer software made stacks of reference books nearly obsolete). I would do the most careful and thorough research I could.

When the project was complete and we all shared our findings, I was astounded at the results. We all came to the same determination: worship is predominantly an action. Worship is not generally something we can do simply from our hearts. It requires more.

The most common Hebrew word for worship means "to bow self down." The most common Greek word translated "worship" means "to kiss (the hand) toward" (i.e., as in blowing a kiss). In fact, according to *Young's Analytical Concordance*, one Greek word that is translated "worshipper" literally means "temple sweeper" (Acts 19:35). Worship in the true scriptural sense is not passive.

There is a time when the Bible says that Jacob leaned on his staff and worshipped the Lord (Genesis 47:31; Hebrews 11:21). However, when looking at the whole of Scripture it becomes obvious that such an uninvolved action is definitely the exception, not the rule. Even a cursory look at worship in the Bible apart from the original languages will bear this concept out.

> ...all the people of Judah and Jerusalem *fell down in worship* before the LORD (2 Chronicles 20:18).
>
> Then they bowed down and *worshipped* the LORD with their faces to the ground (Nehemiah 8:6).
>
> Then he (Job) *fell to the ground in worship* (Job 1:20).
>
> Come, let us *bow down in worship* (Psalm 95:6).
>
> They came to him (Jesus), *clasped His feet and worshipped Him* (Matthew 28:9).
>
> ...*offer your bodies* as living sacrifices, holy and pleasing to God— this is your spiritual act of worship (Romans 12:1).
>
> So he (an unbeliever) will *fall down and worship God*, exclaiming, "God is really among you!" (1 Corinthians 14:25).
>
> ...the twenty-four elders *fall down before Him* who sits on the throne, and worship Him... (Revelation 4:10).

Please understand that worship must originate from the heart, but it cannot be just heart. Worship that is heart alone is passive. However, worship that is action alone is not true worship. God wants heart and action.

Remember the Tabernacle of Moses? God went to great lengths to describe in exact detail how to build the tabernacle. There are entire chapters in the book of Exodus devoted to giving minute details about the building of the tabernacle and its various articles of furniture. Why did God do this? Why spend so much time focusing on the size and shape of the stands for the poles? Why so much time describing such seemingly insignificant details? The fact is that each piece in the tabernacle represented something. I am convinced that such careful planning and details were to help the people to understand that a righteous, holy, all-powerful God did not want His people to be indifferent, lazy or apathetic in their worship of Him.

The Old Testament contains the story of King Amaziah, one of the kings of Judah (2 Chronicles 25:1-28). He ruled the country for twenty-nine years. Verse two summarizes his reign as king: "He did what was right in the eyes of the LORD, *but not wholeheartedly*" (author's emphasis). What an indictment! He did the right things, but not wholeheartedly. If there is one thing that I believe characterizes the current trend in worship within the church in America, it is this: we are not wholehearted for God. We say the right words, sing the right songs — but not wholeheartedly.

I am often guilty of this also. I frequently find myself pondering what things I can do to enhance the worship experience of our congregation. I consider the musical arrangements of our songs, our use of musical dynamics and even the between-song prayers and exhortations. However, after considering all of these things, I am still drawn to one startling and disturbing conclusion: in my attempts to make worship "better" I too often miss out on simply worshipping the Lord.

Over the past several years there has been a proliferation of conferences and seminars teaching people how play musical instruments in such a way as to evoke worship from the congregation, how to make and display banners for worship and even how the use of "body language" can enhance worship. In the midst of all of these "practical" points it is easy to miss the real point of it all: to worship God.

Worship has become a commodity. It has been popularized, arranged, orchestrated, translated, practiced, recorded, reviewed, dissected, analyzed and computerized. In the past few years worship has become one of the most popular topics available for books, conferences, sermons, etc. You can now obtain a complete encyclopedia on worship or go on-line to discover more about worship. It seems that we have reached the point where worship is more something that we examine than something we do. Bob Webber has written a wonderful book, the title of which sums up the point: *Worship is a Verb*. Worship is not something simply for observation. It is something in which we must be *involved*.

Maybe we as the body of Christ should consider setting aside a six-month period of time during which we would dispense with all of the peripheral areas of worship. Each congregation could have one solitary consecrated individual lead them in praise and worship. No hoopla, no hype, just simple whole-hearted worship of God. I realize that this a very impractical idea, but it certainly sounds refreshing to me.

Is it even possible for us to remember the place from which we started? Is it conceivable for us to worship the Lord without a full orchestra sounding forth the latest popular worship songs?

I am reminded of a very sobering passage in the book of Amos: "I hate, I despise your religious feasts; I cannot stand your assemblies. Even though you bring Me burnt offerings and grain offerings, I will not accept them... Away with the noise of your songs! I will not listen to the music of your harps" (Amos 5:21-23).

Who was it who had asked for all of these things (the feasts, the assemblies, the music, etc.) from Israel? Obviously it was God. So why then was He telling them He did not want them any longer? Were they not doing them correctly? On the contrary, it seems to me that by the time Amos brought forth this prophecy the people Israel were very experienced at all of these outward forms of worship. They were probably so good at these things that they could do them without even thinking. Therein lay the problem. The people were more interested in the forms of their worship than in worshipping God.

One of the consistent, main messages of the Old Testament prophets is their strong denunciation of the Israelite "worship" because it had degenerated into external ritualism. They did the right things, but not from their hearts.

Even today it is still easy to fall into this trap. We can become so interested in doing things "right" to get the "right" response that we can miss the whole point of worshipping God.

If you have not already, begin to make it a priority to tune out the "practicals" of worship. Be less concerned with people and things, and instead, focus on the real object of our worship: God Almighty.

One of my favorite Bible passages about worship is Hebrews 12:28; "Therefore, since we are receiving a kingdom that cannot be shaken, let us be thankful, and so worship God acceptably with reverence and awe." It is difficult for me to conceive of offering that "acceptable" worship "with reverence and awe" in a passive sort of way. This type of worship requires true, heart-felt emotion, and that, in turn, involves both heart and action.

Worship: Our Response to God

Definition: Worship is the response of man when he encounters either God or God's actions.

In the introduction I mentioned the various definitions of worship I have encountered over the years. Although brief definitions usually fall short of truly explaining Biblical worship, I believe this one has a lot of merit: Worship is the response of man when he encounters either God or God's actions.

In one of his hymns, John Newton stated it this way:
Weak is the effort of my heart
and cold my warmest thought,
But when I see Thee as Thou art
I'll praise Thee as I ought.

When we encounter the reality of God, true worship is the outcome.

Do you recall the encounter between Elijah and the prophets of Baal on Mt. Carmel? In front of the people of Israel, Elijah issued a challenge to the prophets of the false god Baal. "Get two bulls for us. Let them choose one for themselves, and let them cut it into pieces and put it on the wood but not set fire to it. I will prepare the other bull and put it on the wood but not set fire to it. Then you call on the name of your god, and I will call on the name of the LORD. The god who answers by fire — he is God" (1 Kings 18:23-24). The people agreed.

They did everything exactly as Elijah had said. Baal's prophets prepared their sacrifice and called out to their god. From morning until evening they called out, but nothing happened. Finally, it was Elijah's turn. As if to really prove the point he had his helpers pour large jars of water on his sacrifice. He then stepped up and prayed that the Lord would show the people that He was indeed God. And He did. The bull, the wood, the stones, the soil and even the water were all consumed by the fire.

To me the response of the people really says it all. "When all the people saw this they fell prostrate and cried,

'The LORD — He is God! The LORD — He is God!'" (1 Kings 18:39). No one needed to tell them what to do or how to respond. Worship is the natural response when people encounter God or His actions.

Some time ago I heard a pastor relating an incident of encountering God. This pastor was from a large church, and they had a rather full orchestra that helped lead their times of worship. One day this pastor received a phone call from the head of the music department of a nearby major university. After the introductions the conversation went something like this:

"I understand that you have an orchestra that leads your music on Sunday mornings."

"That's correct."

"I also understand that sometimes they play together with no musical score," (what is commonly referred to as "open worship" or "free worship," playing a chord progression and allowing people to sing spontaneously unto the Lord) "and it sounds good."

Again the pastor responded, "That's correct."

"Well, I'll be honest. I've never heard of anything like that and it really does not make sense to me. What I'd like to do is come to your service sometime and record it and analyze it."

The pastor agreed and they set a date for the man to come and record their music.

On the given Sunday the man arrived and set up his reel-to-reel tape recorder on the front row of the auditorium.

The service began, and the orchestra played. At one point the worship leader had the orchestra play a simple chord progression, and the people sang spontaneously unto the Lord. All of it was captured on tape.

The real capstone on the whole event occurred toward the end of the time of singing. The pastor looked down from the platform and was amazed. The head of the music department of the nearby major university was standing with his hands in the air and tears streaming down his face. No one had witnessed to him, nor had the sermon been preached. The man had encountered God, and his immediate reaction was to worship.

1 Corinthians 14 offers a similar scenario. An unbeliever comes into the church and people are speaking forth prophetically. He is convicted by their words, and he realizes that God is there. His response is similar to the man above. "So he will fall down and worship God, exclaiming, 'God is really among you!'" (1 Corinthians 14:24-25). In this scene Paul does not suggest that someone will need to show the man scriptural precedent for bowing in worship. It is the obvious response.

In his book, *Whatever Happened to Worship?*, A.W. Tozer relates a fascinating account about Blaise Pascal, the famous 17th century French scientist.

> (Pascal) is often classed as one the of the greatest thinkers of all time. He was considered a genius in mathematics, and his scientific inquiry was broad. He was a philosopher and a

writer. But best of all, he experienced a personal, overwhelming encounter with God one night that changed his life.

Pascal wrote on a piece of paper a brief account of his experience, folded the paper and kept it in a pocket close to his heart, apparently as a reminder of what he had felt. Those who attended him at his death found the worn, creased paper. In Pascal's own hand it read:

"From half-past ten at night to about half-after midnight — fire! O God of Abraham, God of Isaac, God of Jacob — not the god of the philosophers and the wise. The God of Jesus Christ who can only be known in the ways of the Gospel: security - feeling - peace - joy - tears of joy. Amen."

Were these the expressions of a fanatic, an extremist?

No. Pascal's mind was one of the greatest. But the living God had broken through and beyond all that was human and intellectual and philosophical. The astonished Pascal could only describe in one word the visitation in his spirit: "Fire!"

Understand that this was not a statement in sentences for others to read. It was the ecstatic utterance of a yielded man during two awesome hours in the presence of his God.

> There was no human engineering or ma-
> nipulation there. There was only wonder and
> awe and adoration wrought by the presence of
> the Holy Spirit as Pascal worshipped. [Tozer, A.W.,
> *Whatever Happened To Worship?* (Camp Hill, Penn., Vine
> Books, 1985), pp. 90-91.]

The Bible is replete with similar illustrations of man's reaction to God. The gospels of Matthew, Mark and John all relate the incident of Jesus walking on the water. By the time this happened the disciples had been with Jesus for some time. They had even seen Him perform numerous miracles. However, when the disciples saw Jesus walking across the water something happened in their hearts and minds. They suddenly realized this was not just an espe-cially gifted man — this was God. Their response? "Then those who were in the boat *worshipped* him, saying, 'Truly you are the Son of God'" (Matthew 14:33).

For us today, even if we have not had an extraordi-nary encounter with God, we have all witnessed the reality of God and His works. "We cannot worship rightly until we recapture, as the principle element of worship, the over-whelming sense of awe and reverence in the presence of God" [Bailey, Robert W., *New Ways in Christian Worship* (Nashville, Broadman, 1981), pp. 35-36]. We have seen the wonder of God in His creation (Romans 1:20). We have experienced the acts of the Lord in His redemptive sacrifice. We have all "seen" enough of God that worship should be our ongoing response. The late Robert G. Lee said, "If I had a thousand heads and each head had a thousand tongues and each tongue spoke a thousand dialects and I could speak for eternity, I still could not praise Jesus sufficiently."

Throughout the Bible, and even in our age, as men encounter God or see His mighty hand at work, the instantaneous response is worship. There is no need for them to consider their actions. They realize they are in the presence of the Almighty, and the only appropriate response is worship.

Worship: Giving to God

Definition: True Worship Is Costly

The concept of *giving* to God as a part of worship can be seen throughout the whole of the Bible. It seems to be almost a given that worship will cost something.

The entire Old Testament sacrificial system was set up as a means of giving to the Lord. People brought their animals, which they had spent time and energy nurturing and caring for, to offer as a sacrifice to God. In fact, by the time of Jesus this system had become very refined. People making the pilgrimage to Jerusalem for the Passover celebration no longer needed to bring their own animals for the sacrifices. They could simply bring along some extra cash and purchase the appropriate sacrificial animal right at the temple. It made the process much easier than trying to corral a young lamb all the way to Jerusalem.

Either way, however, their worship still cost them something. It was either the time and effort of raising the animal or the actual monetary value of purchasing an animal for the sacrifice. Their worship offered something of value to God.

King David understood the principle of worship being costly. Because David had sinned by taking a census of Israel, God caused a plague to come upon the people. A total of 70,000 people died as a result. David was devastated over the carnage, and cried out to the Lord. Because of this, the prophet, Gad, came to David and said to him, "Go up and build an altar to the LORD on the threshing floor of Araunah the Jebusite" (2 Samuel 24:18).

So David went to Araunah and offered to purchase his threshing floor in order to build the necessary altar. Araunah, apparently flattered that his property had been chosen for such a sacred event, offered to give David the threshing floor. He also offered oxen for the sacrifice, and threshing sledges, and ox yokes for the wood on which to burn the sacrifice. Araunah said, "O King, Araunah gives all this to the king... May the Lord your God accept you" (2 Samuel 24:23).

David, however, knew better. He understood that simply taking something from someone else to offer to God was not acceptable. David's response to Araunah was simple, "No, I insist on paying you for it. I will not sacrifice to the Lord my God burnt offerings that cost me nothing" (2 Samuel 24:24). David refused to offer up a sacrifice in which he had no real investment.

Because David understood and practiced this principle, the end result was that he paid for the items, offered the sacrifice and the plague was stopped. Would God have ended the plague if David had simply accepted the items as gifts from Araunah? Of course there is no way to tell for certain, but my guess is that He probably would not have ended it. In order to be truly acceptable, worship must cost us something.

Although we no longer offer burnt offerings in our modern society, the word "sacrifice" has come to mean "giving up of something for the sake of another." This very fact should indicate that the original concept had to do with giving up something. It was truly a sacrifice.

Look at it from a different perspective. If someone were to give you a gift, would you rather receive diamond earrings or plastic ones? A rusted out Pinto or a brand-new Rolls Royce? The same is true for God. He doesn't want cheap imitations or leftovers. He wants our very best. And please realize that I am not even talking just about finances.

The Bible is replete with references to giving to God. Beyond just the monetary aspects, Scripture repeatedly refers to giving *glory* and *honor* and *thanks* to the Lord.

Another example in our society is time. We never seem to have enough time to do things that we know are essential. Time to go to church. Time to spend in prayer. Time to read and study the Word. Time is valuable. When we become possessive of our time, refusing to offer it to God, there will be no true worship. Insisting that my time belongs to me is no different than insisting that any material possession truly belongs to me. However, willingly offering our time to the Lord is worship.

Luke records the story of the woman who broke the very expensive alabaster jar of perfume and poured it on Jesus (Luke 7:36-50). The Pharisees were aghast that He would allow such a sinful woman to touch Him. Jesus simply told them a story about forgiveness and love, and asked them a question. He then equated her costly sacrifice, including the jar of perfume, her time and her affection, with her love for Him.

The reality is that to Jesus, she was demonstrating true worship. It was costly. It cost her money: perhaps her entire life's savings to purchase the jar of perfume. It cost her time: to seek out Jesus and spend time at His feet. It cost her dignity: to wash His feet with her tears and her hair, and to kiss them repeatedly. And from Jesus' reaction it would appear that her worship was exactly right.

The costliness itself is not ultimately what God is after. He owns everything we have. Neither you nor I can give Him something from our possessions that He does not already have. So what's the point? Very simply, our willingness to give costly worship is an indication of our heart attitude. Jesus said it this way, "For where your treasure is, there your heart will be also" (Matthew 6:21). When we are willing to give the Lord things that we possess we are telling Him that He is worth more to us than those things.

The origin of the English word "worship" illustrates this. The word was originally "worthship." It was used to address or describe someone of importance, someone worthy of honor or respect. This concept is still used in Great Britain in reference to certain dignitaries: His Worship, the Mayor of ____. It doesn't mean that the mayor is to be worshipped, but that he is worthy of honor. His position gives him worth in the sight of the people. In that light, what is God worth to us?

Ultimately, the Lord is most interested in our hearts. He does not want us to give Him worship in a begrudging sort of way. Scripture says that God loves a cheerful giver (2 Corinthians 9:7). In saying this, Paul seems to imply that God has some other type of attitude toward someone who gives in a less-than-cheerful way. He is not interested in just the act of giving, unless it is an expression of our heart.

Do you remember when God asked Abraham to offer Isaac as a sacrifice? Isaac was Abraham's long-awaited son. He had waited for years for the Lord's promise to be fulfilled, and now the promise was reality. After such a lengthy time of anticipation, to finally have a son must have been like a dream come true for Abraham. Isaac could easily have become the center of Abraham's attention. After all, through this boy-child the Lord had promised to bless all the peoples of the earth. This son was the beginning of a chapter in history that was unprecedented.

Then God spoke the unthinkable. "Take your son...to the region of Moriah. Sacrifice him there as a burnt offering..." (Genesis 22:2).

No indication is given in the text that Abraham even slightly balked at the request. In fact it says that he left "early the next morning." Abraham went to the designated mountain and prepared to sacrifice Isaac. He built an altar, arranged the wood for burning, bound Isaac and laid him on the altar on top of the wood. Just as Abraham was preparing to slay his son, the angel of the Lord stopped him.

"Do not lay a hand on the boy," he said. "Do not do anything to him. Now I know that you fear God, because you have not withheld from me your son, your only son" (Genesis 22:12). The Living Bible's rendering of the middle section of this passage is particularly pointed: "...for I know that God is first in your life..." God was not as interested in the actual sacrifice itself as He was in Abraham's heart.

Giving to the Lord out of a heart filled with gratitude and praise is truly an act of worship that God enjoys. Are we willing to sacrifice our time, our finances and even whatever is most precious to us to our most worthy God?

To worship is to quicken the conscience by the holiness of God, to feed the mind with the truth of God, to purge the imagination by the beauty of God, to open the heart to the love of God, to devote the will to the purpose of God.

William Temple, the late Archbishop of Canterbury

Because this definition is rather lengthy, the following five chapters will expand on this concept. Each chapter will look at one of the five parts of this definition.

Worship: To Quicken the Conscience by the Holiness of God

Definition: To worship is to quicken the conscience by the holiness of God...

I remember part of a sermon I heard as a little boy. The pastor was relating several Scriptures but then, to emphasize his point, he shared an old Indian proverb. "Conscience is like a three-pointed stone inside of a man. The more he goes against his conscience the more the points wear off the stone." The pastor went on to explain that eventually, if we violate our conscience often enough, it will no longer effect us.

I have found from both my experience and my study of God's Word that this is true. However, I have also found that a realization of the holiness of God will sharpen the points of the stone.

The prophet Isaiah was apparently one of the most godly, holy men of his time. If you study his life and his words you will find this to be true. However, one day Isaiah encountered the holiest Being in the universe, and he suddenly became aware of his own unholiness.

> In the year that King Uzziah died, I saw the Lord seated on a throne, high and exalted, and the train of his robe filled the temple. Above him were seraphs, each with six wings: With two wings they covered their faces, with two they covered their feet, and with two they were flying. And they were calling to one another: "Holy, holy, holy is the LORD Almighty; the whole earth is full of his glory." At the sound of their voices the doorposts and thresholds shook and the temple was filled with smoke. "Woe to me!" I cried. "I am ruined! For I am a man of unclean lips, and I live among a people of unclean lips, and my eyes have seen the King, the LORD Almighty" (Isaiah 6:1-5).

Please understand that Isaiah was a good guy. He was not part of the Mob. He did not rob banks. He was not involved in the pornography business. He did not worship false gods. He loved the Lord. But encountering the holiness of God made him suddenly aware of his own sinfulness. Look again at his response. "Woe to me! I am ruined!"

Throughout Scripture prophets consistently use one of two words to begin their prophetic utterances: "blessed" or "woe." If they were speaking affirming words from God they started by blessing the hearers. However, if the words were harsh, if they were rebuking the hearers, they started with "woe." Please realize that this is not just a cute little word with which to start off a negative statement. It actually has the connotation of a curse (as opposed to a blessing). This was serious. And Isaiah used this word on himself: "Woe to me!"

He went on to say "I am ruined!" Other versions say things like, "My doom is sealed," "I am undone," or "I am lost." This was not a game for Isaiah. When he beheld the Lord, he realized anew his own sinfulness, so much so that he was certain that God would destroy him. When we encounter the holiness of the Lord our conscience is quickened; made alive.

Some years ago I heard noted author and teacher Judson Cornwall talking about this same subject. He mentioned that he had recently been having lunch at a very nice, dimly lit restaurant. During the meal he had spilled some sauce on his tie. Using his napkin and a little water from his glass, he felt he had pretty well removed the spot from his tie. However, when he went into the more brightly lighted lobby he realized that he had not completely eliminated the spot. He proceeded to the rest room and worked a bit more on the stain. Confident he had completely removed the spot this time he left the restaurant. Unfortunately, when he got outside in the full light of the midday sun, he realized the spot still remained. In reality, the spot was there the entire time. It simply became more obvious as the intensity of the light increased.

Dr. Cornwall went on to explain that much the same thing can happen to us when we encounter God. As we come into contact with the holiness of the Lord we realize, just like Isaiah, that we are sinful. The more of His holiness we realize, the more convicted we become. Our conscience is quickened by the holiness of God.

The great reformer, Martin Luther, was an interesting character. He entered the ministry because he was afraid that if he did not God would kill him. Prior to entering the monastery he had distinguished himself in law school. He had shown that he was a brilliant man long before becoming a priest. In fact he showed such promise as a lawyer that his father vehemently opposed his decision to enter the ministry. The younger Luther did ultimately enter the monastery and studied hard and faithfully.

Finally the day came when he would perform his first mass. He had carefully prepared his sermon. He had been through each part of the mass again and again. He knew exactly what to say and how to say it. He knew every part forward and backward. He was ready. However, when the moment came for the Eucharist, Luther froze. He simply could not speak.

Throughout his study in the Roman Catholic Church Luther had been taught that the bread and the wine actually become the body and blood of the Lord Jesus Christ. The term that Catholics use is transubstantiation: the bread and the wine literally turn into the body and blood of Jesus. Whether or not you agree with this teaching is immaterial. To Martin Luther, what he held in his hands was the actual Body of Jesus. He suddenly became so aware that he, a sinful mortal, was handling the Body of the holy Son of God, Jesus, that he could not speak. He froze. He had not forgotten the words. He had encountered God, and realized anew his own sinfulness.

One evening Jesus and His disciples were in a boat crossing to the other side of the lake (Matthew 8:18, 23-27; Mark 4:35-41; Luke 8:22-25). Suddenly a fierce storm came up. The wind blew and waves swept over the boat so that it was nearly swamped. Through all of this commotion Jesus slept in the back of the boat. Finally, the disciples, obviously a bit afraid, went to Him and said, "Teacher, don't You care if we drown?" (Mark 4:38).

Keep in mind that several of these men were very experienced fishermen. They had spent a large portion of their lives in boats on this very lake. If they were afraid of drowning in this storm, it must have been a major storm.

Do you recall Jesus' reaction to the situation? "He got up, rebuked the wind and said to the waves, 'Quiet! Be still!' Then the wind died down and it was completely calm" (Mark 4:39).

The response of the disciples to this whole scenario is amazing. "They were terrified..." Just a few moments earlier they had been afraid of drowning. It looked as if their lives were coming to an end, and they were scared. Now, when they realized anew that they were face to face with the Lord, they were *terrified*. They understood that they were sinful men, and that this was the holy God. Their consciences were quickened.

Understanding and experiencing the holiness of God will always quicken, or renew, our consciences just like it did for Isaiah, Martin Luther and Jesus' disciples.

Worship: To Feed the Mind with the Truth of God

*Definition: To worship is to... feed the
mind with the truth of God...*

S ome time ago I heard well-known teacher Terry Law
speaking at a conference. He was talking about the
Word of God, and during his message he referred to Psalm
107:20: "He sent forth His Word and healed them." Terry
then posed the question, "Is this talking about the written
Word or Jesus, the Word made flesh?" Of the few hundred

people in attendance there were those who were absolutely certain that one or the other was correct. Terry said the correct answer to the question is "Yes." He went on to explain that we must understand that the two are inseparable, the Word of God is the Word of God, regardless of the form.

In John 14:6, Jesus told His followers that *He* is *the truth.* Later, in John 17:17, He is praying for His disciples. He asks the Father to "sanctify them by the truth; *Your Word* is *truth.*" Since Jesus will soon be no longer visibly with them it seems obvious that His prayer here is referring to the spoken/written Word of God. Both Jesus, the Word made flesh, and the spoken/written Word are truth, and have power in our lives. "...for You have exalted above all things Your name and *Your Word*" (Psalm 138:2b).

The written Word of God is as life-transforming as a personal encounter with Jesus. Unfortunately, because it is just ink on paper we often place it on a much lower plane in our society. Oh, for the Church to have a revelation of the power and significance of the written Word of God!

The book of Nehemiah relates a fascinating account of God's people realizing the value of His written Word. The rebuilding of the wall around Jerusalem had been completed. The people had begun to return to inhabit the city. After this process happened the Scripture says: "All the people assembled as one man in the square before the Water Gate. They told Ezra the scribe to bring out the Book of the Law of Moses, which the LORD had commanded for

Israel" (Nehemiah 8:1). So Ezra did, and he began to read from the Book of the Law. "He read it aloud from daybreak till noon as he faced the square before the Water Gate in the presence of the men, women and others who could understand. And all the people listened attentively to the Book of the Law" (Nehemiah 8:3). They "listened attentively" from "daybreak till noon"?! What value they placed on the Word of God.

"Ezra the scribe stood on a high wooden platform built for the occasion... Ezra opened the book. All the people could see him because he was standing above them; and as he opened it, the people all stood up. Ezra praised the LORD, the great God; and all the people lifted their hands and responded, 'Amen! Amen!' Then they bowed down and worshipped the LORD with their faces to the ground" (Nehemiah 8:4-6). How different from our normal reaction today. Public reading of Scripture today is usually met with a much less enthusiastic response than this. We must begin to realize the immense value in the written Word of God.

Too often today this idea is almost completely missing. In many churches more emphasis is placed on experience than on the already written Truth.

I recently attended a three-day conference that was a bit different than my normal experience. The people were predominantly from one particular denomination. Although theologically I did not fully agree with everything that happened, I learned some very profound truths. However, the thing that really stood out to me was the reverence of those people for the Word of God. These were seemingly not just words on a printed page, or spoken from the platform. They were the Words of the Lord. The words were cherished and savored. They were taken to heart, not just listened to.

We would all do well to learn this type of reverence for the holy Scriptures, the inspired Word of God. We must learn to say with the psalmist: "I have chosen the way of truth; *I have set my heart on Your laws*" (Psalm 119:30).

This is not just a side issue with God. Realizing the value of the truth of His Word is a priority. When Pontius Pilate was questioning Jesus, the Lord made this statement: "...for this I came into the world, to testify to the truth. Everyone on the side of truth listens to me" (John 18:37). One of the main reasons Jesus came to earth was to "testify to the truth." How should we then value that truth?

We must begin to understand that feeding our minds with the Word, in and of itself, is an act of worship.

Allow me a few moments to offer some balance to this. Not long ago I was invited to teach a worship seminar at a rather traditional denominational church. The man coordinating the seminar had been the full-time minister of music at that church for over ten years. When I arrived he mentioned to me that there was one main reason why he wanted to do the seminar. He said that the mindset of the people of the church was that the sermon is worship. To their way of thinking the sermon equals worship, and worship equals the sermon. Period. There are no other variables. The singing, offering, etc., are all just preliminaries. The real high point of worship is the message. He was hoping that I could help the congregation to understand that although this is important, it is not all there is to worship.

It is interesting to note that the two denominational stories that I just shared are both from the same denomination. What is a very great strength (reverence for the Word) can become a weakness if carried too far. I am not picking on people from a particular denominational background. The same thing can happen even in independent churches.

A while back I heard about a well-known independent pentecostal/charismatic teacher who regularly refers to the music/worship leader as "the preliminary man." He uses this phrase because to him the most important aspect of the service is the sermon. Excuse my bluntness, but when we begin to view the act of people wholeheartedly worshipping the Lord through the medium of song as a preliminary, we have totally missed the heart of God.

The key word here is balance. Unfortunately we usually tend to stray too far in one direction or the other. We must never lose sight of the fact that feeding our minds with the truth of God, His holy Word, in and of itself, is an act of worship. However, it is not the only act of worship. There is far more to worshipping the Lord than this alone.

Worship: To Purge the Imagination by the Beauty of God

Definition: To worship is to... purge the imagination by the beauty of God...

A cts 2:25 tells us that "David said about Him: 'I saw the Lord always before me. Because He is at my right hand, I will not be shaken.'" What an interesting statement. "...I *saw* the Lord..." Did David literally *see* the Lord? Of course not. However, because he chose to perceive God all around him David was not afraid even in life-threatening situations. He filled the frame of his mind with the Lord, and there was no room left for doubt or despair. We too can purge our imagination by focusing on God.

In our western culture we have less and less need to use our imagination. Previously, television and movies made our imagination less needed. With the advent of "virtual reality," and its ever increasing applications, there is almost nothing left for us to imagine. We can experience practically everything.

The only time most people really use their imagination is for the wrong reasons. They think about what they would do if they had as much money as Microsoft boss, Bill Gates. They imagine what it would be like to be as attractive as their favorite movie star. They wonder what it would be like to be married to someone else. Greed. Covetousness. Lust. All the wrong uses for imagination, but, unfortunately, the most common ones.

This mindset of non-use of our imagination so permeates our culture that it has even become a part of the Church. In his book, *Worship is a Verb*, Bob Webber talks about how we view God. He writes, "Our approach to God is intellectual and scientific on one extreme and excessively 'buddy-buddy' on the other; both are sorely lacking in imagination." [Webber, Robert E., *Worship is a Verb* (Waco, Word, 1985)]. Most people seldom use their God-given imagination to imagine what God is like. Instead they fill their imagination with all the wrong things, things that need to be purged from them.

Scripture gives us a clear directive in this area. "Finally, brothers, whatever is true, whatever is noble, whatever is right, whatever is pure, whatever is lovely, whatever is admirable — if anything is excellent or praiseworthy — think about such things" (Philippians 4:8). I realize that this verse is referring to many things on which our minds can dwell. However, think for a moment about the attributes mentioned. "True," "noble," "right," "pure," "lovely," "admirable," "excellent," "praiseworthy." What one Being (there's a hint) epitomizes all of these attributes to the highest possible degree? God, of course. "...think about such things." We can think about the Lord.

When we begin to use our God-given imagination in thinking about God our perceptions of Him often expand. When we release our minds to view the Lord as true and right and pure and lovely and admirable and excellent and praiseworthy, He becomes more wonderful than our usual flat, mundane perception of Him. As we go beyond our intellectual assessment of God, or our buddy-buddy thinking, we can begin to really "see" His holiness, His majesty, His power. When this happens we are often astounded by the beauty of God. Something happens to us as people, and to our imagination. We become more like Him.

"But we know that when He appears, we shall be like Him, for we shall see Him as He is" (1 John 3:2b). The more that I get to know God the more I am convinced that this is not just a promise for the future, but is true, in part, even now. In context, this passage is obviously referring to the second coming of Jesus. However, it clearly tells us that the reason we shall be like Him is because "we shall see Him as He is." As we behold Him, we are changed to be like Him.

One of my favorite songwriters is Mark Altrogge, a pastor in Indiana, Pennsylvania. Many of his songs have tremendously and positively influenced my walk with the Lord. In his song, "The Love of a Holy God," Mark alludes to beholding God: "I'm ravished by one glance from Your loving eyes." While some have questioned the use of the word "ravished" I personally think it is perfect. It reminds me of Isaiah's experience of seeing the Lord in Isaiah 6. Remember his words? "I am ruined..." There is something about beholding the beauty of God that rips us apart and puts us back together even better than we were, all at the same time. Things are removed from our thinking. Our imagination is purged.

I am not suggesting that through a single encounter with the Lord your thought life will be forever perfect. It is possible, but not normal. My experience has been that the more I gaze on the beauty of the Lord the more I am conformed to His image. "...we shall be like Him, for we shall see Him..." Filling the frame of our imagination with God, just like David did, leaves no room for anything else.

In our society there is an intense battle for the mind. Ungodly forces, both human and spiritual, desire to take control of our minds. We have all heard the old adage that our minds are like computers. If we put garbage in, we get garbage out. However, when we focus our minds on the beauty of the Lord, the other thoughts begin to fade away.

The writer of the book of Hebrews tells us to "fix our eyes on Jesus..." (Hebrews 12:2). Can we actually *see* Jesus with our eyes? Again, the answer is no. However, we can focus our thoughts on the wonder of our God. We can make David's prayer in Psalm 27 our own prayer. "One thing I ask of the LORD, this is what I seek: that I may dwell in the house of the LORD all the days of my life, *to gaze upon the beauty of the LORD* and to seek Him in His temple" (Psalm 27:4).

We can purge our imagination by gazing upon the beauty of the Lord. When we do this we are offering our minds to the Lord, and He receives this simple act of worship.

Worship: To Open the Heart to the Love of God

Definition: To worship is to... open the heart to the love of God...

The day that I came into the kingdom was when I realized the truth of John 3:16, not as a general statement, but for me. "For God so loved the world..." Truth. But one day I realized He loved *me*. *I* was included in the world, and He loved me that much also. I opened my heart to that love, and I was born-again.

The fact is that coming into a saving relationship with God through Jesus Christ is a prerequisite for worship. It is only as we truly begin to open our hearts to His love that we can really worship Him. If we are honest, however, we realize that we cannot simply stop there. We must continually open our hearts to the love of God.

When I was in seminary, one of the professors asked how many of us had had their lives radically changed when they began to realize the fullness of the love of God. Almost everyone in the class raised his hand. There is something life-changing about truly opening the heart to God's love. And simply receiving that love can be an act of worship.

The apostle Paul said it this way, "I pray that you, being rooted and established in love, may have power, together with all the saints, to grasp how wide and long and high and deep is the love of Christ, and to know this love that surpasses knowledge — that you may be filled to the measure of all the fullness of God" (Ephesians 3:17b-19). Receiving the love of the Lord causes us to be filled up "to the measure of all the fullness of God."

This concept of receiving God's love can be one of the most difficult things for us as Christians, especially after we have known the Lord for any length of time. Most people who came into the Kingdom of God later in life point to His love as the reason for their "decision." They realized, just like I did, that God Almighty loved them.

However, after several years of walking with the Lord we often have difficulty believing that God could still love us. After all, we reason, we have been a part of His Kingdom for a long time, and we should be more straightened out than we are. In the current vernacular, we should have more of our act together.

We often feel the way Paul must have felt when he wrote Romans 7: "For what I do is not the good I want to do; no, the evil I do not want to do — this I keep on doing" (Romans 7:19). And in the midst of that struggle we cannot fathom how God could possibly love us. We too often refuse to open our hearts to His love, and, hence, there is no worship.

Further along in the same chapter Paul sinks even further. "What a wretched man I am! Who will rescue me from this body of death?" (Romans 7:24). He finally had to come to the point where he simply opened his heart to the love of God. There is no other cure for sin. He simply repented and received God's love.

And what truth and reality Paul found when he did that! "For I am convinced that neither death nor life, neither angels nor demons, neither the present nor the future, nor any powers, neither height nor depth, nor anything else in all creation, will be able to separate us from the love of God that is in Christ Jesus our Lord" (Romans 8:38-39). Just one chapter later, Paul is a changed man. And it is because he opened his heart to the love of his God.

Regardless of how long we have walked with the Lord there is something refreshing about receiving God's love anew. In the last chapter I mentioned Mark Altrogge's song, "The Love of a Holy God." Another line in that song says, "I'm ruined for this world for I've tasted Your love, the love of a holy God." The fact that God is so holy and yet still loves sinful creatures like us makes His love even more wonderful. All the treasures of this world pale in comparison.

Opening our hearts to the love of the Lord is not just a New Testament concept either. As I searched the Scriptures about God's love in the context of worship, I was amazed at what I found in the Old Testament. I looked at over 80 different passages just in the book of Psalms that spoke very clearly about the Lord's love in the context of worship. There were some that called on the Lord to show His love, but I did not count those. I only considered the ones that declared His love, or thanked Him for His love.

Here are a few of my favorites:

How priceless is your unfailing love! Both high and low among men find refuge in the shadow of your wings (Psalm 36:7).

Because your love is better than life, my lips will glorify you (Psalm 63:3).

But from everlasting to everlasting the LORD's love is with those who fear him (Psalm 103:17).

For great is your love, higher than the heavens; your faithfulness reaches to the skies (Psalm 108:4).

It is as we begin to truly open our hearts to that love that we find a fullness and richness in our worship.

I have found that too often Christians act as though God is sitting up in heaven just waiting for them to mess up (sin, miss the mark, etc.) so He can beat them over the head. This image is far removed from the loving heavenly Father of the Bible. Jesus said that God loves us as much as God loved Him (John 17:23).

Please understand that God despises sin. Sin is heinous. It is the thing that sent Jesus to the cross. There is no acceptable excuse for sin. But there is forgiveness. "If You, O LORD, kept a record of sins, O Lord, who could stand? But with You there is forgiveness..." (Psalm 130:3-4a). And that forgiveness is in the form of the love of God.

When we learn that the Lord still loves us, regardless of where we are or what we have done, we will find a freedom for worship that will not come any other way. As we open our hearts to the greatness of His love, we are, in fact, worshipping Him.

Worship: To Devote the Will to the Purpose of God

Definition: To worship is to... devote the will to the purpose of God.

This concept is one of the most overlooked aspects of worship. Subsequent chapters will go into more detail about this idea, but I will endeavor to offer a few thoughts here based on this definition.

We have already looked at Isaiah's encounter with the Lord a couple of times in this book. However, because it is such a classic example of worship, and depicts so many different aspects about worship, we will look there once again.

Amidst the seraphs intense worship of God, Isaiah becomes convicted of his own unholiness. The Lord had made provision for the cleansing. "Then one of the seraphs flew to me with a live coal in his hand, which he had taken with tongs from the altar. With it he touched my mouth and said, 'See, this has touched your lips; your guilt is taken away and your sin atoned for'" (Isaiah 6:6-7).

Immediately following this the Lord called out, "Whom shall I send? And who will go for us?" Please note that there had been no mention of "going" prior to this. Nothing was said about a mission. All that had happened was worship, conviction and cleansing. However, even before he knew all of the facts Isaiah cried out, "Here am I. Send me!" (Isaiah 6:8). He did not ask questions. He was seemingly not interested in when or why or how or even where. Whatever the Lord wanted was acceptable. Isaiah's will was devoted to God and in that simple act of devotion, the Lord received worship.

As we encounter the reality of God, questions about His desires for us fade. We simply begin to want what He wants. And to the Lord there is no higher form of worship. Saying, "Yes" to His desires will bring Him ultimate glory.

As I travel I have encountered numerous churches that have a banner over the door leading to the outside. The banner reads, "You are now entering your mission field." I even heard of one church that used a slightly different twist. Their banner read, "Welcome to the Evangelism Department." When people begin to catch a vision for souls where they live they will almost automatically begin to pray for and share with those people. What these banners are really saying is, "It is now time for you to devote your will to the purpose of God. Whatever the Lord asks of you, wherever He places you, diligently pursue His purposes for you."

We must cultivate this type of mindset in the Church. I have heard numerous Christians say something like, "I'll do whatever the Lord wants as long as it isn't _____." You fill in the blank. God is not interested in our restrictions on His plan. He wants us with no reservations.

"...whatever you do, do it all for the glory of God" (1 Corinthians 10:31).

Devoting our wills to the purposes of God is not usually what we think of as worship. However, it seems obvious that if we truly want to honor Him, then devoting ourselves to His plans will bring Him glory and honor. We can worship God by wholeheartedly fulfilling His desires.

Worship: A Way of Life

*Definition: The essence of worship is that
God is preeminent all of the time,
not just on Sunday morning.*

In our culture it is common for us to relegate worship to being only a Sunday-morning activity. It is the singing, prayer, reflection, Word-oriented things we do during our Sunday-morning "worship services." Nothing more.

I find it interesting that one of the most often quoted worship passages is frequently misunderstood. John 4:23

tells us that God is seeking "worshippers." It does not say that He is looking for "worship." Instead of using the word which refers to the action, Jesus used the word referring to the person. A worshipper does not just offer an occasional sacrifice of praise through song. A true worshipper lives a life of worship in all that he or she says and does.

In his tape series, *Worship: A Biblical View*, Charles Stanley says this: "If our purpose in life is to glorify God (keep in mind that we have seven days per week and 24 hours per day or 168 hours per week) isn't it ridiculous for us to think that God would be happy with one hour on Sunday morning? 'All I have time for, O sovereign, righteous, omnipotent, omniscient, omnipresent, forgiving, eternal God is one hour per week.'"

The truth is that worship, if it is indeed our main purpose in life, should permeate all that we do and say. Well-known theologian G. Campbell Morgan once said that the worship of the sanctuary is meaningless unless it is preceded by six days of worship as a way of life. If we truly understand the grace of God, this statement is a bit strong. Nevertheless, it has a lot of merit. We cannot live our lives any way that we want to for six days, and then come in to church on Sunday morning and expect to fully worship the Lord. It simply will not work.

In their book, *Worship: Rediscovering the Missing Jewel*, Ronald Allen and Gordon Borror state it this way; "The real factor in worship is a heart desire for God; the reason it fails to occur in the pew is because it fails to occur in the daily routine of living" [Allen, Ronald B. and Borror, Gordon L., *Worship: Rediscovering the Missing Jewel* (Portland, OR, Multnomah, 1982), p. 24].

Ultimately, our Sunday morning experience of worship should be the culmination of six days of worship lived in our lives.

"So whether you eat or drink or whatever you do, do it all for the glory of God" (1 Corinthians 10:31). "Whatever you do, work at it with all your heart, as working for the Lord, not for men" (Colossians 3:23). When we begin to understand these and similar passages in the Bible, we realize that all that we do should be worship unto God.

"When the heart is set upon God, true worship will not depend upon outward stimulus, it will be in constant progress" [Allen, Ronald B. and Borror, Gordon L., *Worship: Rediscovering the Missing Jewel* (Portland, OR, Multnomah, 1982), p. 23].

Brother Lawrence, a medieval monk who coined the phrase "practicing the presence of God," alludes to the idea that when it was time for prayer at the monastery it frequently interrupted his worship of God in washing the dishes. We need that type of understanding of worship in our own lives.

Romans 12:1 says that we are to *offer our bodies* "as living sacrifices, holy and pleasing to God — this is your spiritual act of worship." Giving ourselves, wholly and completely unto the Lord is worship. I like to think of doing that on a daily basis. Would it make a difference in your life if you thought like that? Suppose that for the next week, each day when you get out of bed you say, "Lord, today I am Yours. Wherever I go, whatever I do, I want my life to bring praise and honor unto You. Wherever I am, whether at home, on my job, in school, in the marketplace, I dedicate all that I do to Your glory. Lord, let my life be worship unto You." If you really did that do you suppose it would make a difference in your life?

What if everyone in your church did that? What if from Monday through Saturday each person made it a point to dedicate themselves to doing "all for the glory of God," and then all came together on Sunday morning to corporately offer up their lives of worship? Do you suppose there might be just a bit of a difference in the corporate worship experience? Of course there would. But for this to really happen we must first understand that worship is to permeate our lives.

Worship: Doing unto Others

*Definition: Real worship will portray
the love of God in practical ways
to the world for which He died.*

A number of years ago two friends unknowingly challenged me by their provocative comments. One told me that he felt there appeared to be four main themes within the body of Christ today. These are world evangelization, prayer and revival, praise and worship and social justice. Each of these has a solid scriptural basis and a large following in the church today.

My friend observed that he could see the first three themes; evangelism, prayer and worship, being brought into a degree of unity through events like prayer-and-praise marches. However, the fourth area, social justice, seems somewhat distant from the other three.

Later, a second friend of mine shared that he had seen a connection in Scripture between worship and social justice. In fact, he felt that the Lord had spoken to his heart to say: "The fragrance of worship is justice." He understood this to mean, in part, that the two are so closely linked that they cannot be separated.

I found this concept interesting, but I was quite skeptical. I've heard a lot of people share something that "God told them" that, quite honestly, was not scriptural. It was simply another theory devised to satisfy our desire for something new and improved, even from God's Word. Because of this, I decided to research the relationship between worship and social justice for myself. I was amazed at what I found.

From a biblical perspective, the Lord appears to be far more interested in our acts of kindness; our deeds of social justice, than in our songs of praise. More than just our Sunday morning lip-service, He wants our lives.

I came across a section in the first chapter of Isaiah, verses 10-16, which speaks about the heart attitude in worship. For several years I had taught from this portion of Scripture. God is lambasting His people for going through the motions of worship, but missing the real heart motivation.

As I began to study this social justice/worship relationship I discovered these passages anew. I realized that I had never really noticed the words that follow. "Seek justice, encourage the oppressed. Defend the cause of the fatherless, plead the case of the widow" (Isaiah 1:17). At the end of God's tirade against His people about what was wrong with their worship He tells them to "seek justice." He says they should "encourage the oppressed." God charges them to "defend the cause of the fatherless." Even to "plead the case of the widow." Did I miss a curve somewhere, or is the Lord relating these two things, worship and social justice, to one another? Coincidence? Read on.

Jeremiah also pronounces a strong word of correction to the people of Israel. He tells them that when they come to worship God they should not trust in their actions, nor their words, nor even that they are worshipping in the temple of the Lord. He tells them to change their ways and actions, and "deal with each other justly..."! (Jeremiah 7:1-8).

"I hate, I despise your religious feasts; I cannot stand your assemblies. Even though you bring Me burnt offerings and grain offerings, I will not accept them. Though you bring choice fellowship offerings, I will have no regard for them. Away with the noise of your songs! I will not listen to the music of your harps. But let justice roll on like a river, righteousness like a never-failing stream!" (Amos 5:21-24).

There it is again! It *appears* that the Lord is saying that, unless we are performing deeds of kindness, unless there are acts of justice within our lives, our songs of praise are meaningless. God is far more interested in our lives than our words. We can come into our church buildings singing songs of praise, but if our ears are deaf to those who cry out for justice, is it really of any value? "To obey is better than sacrifice" (1 Samuel 15:22).

I once heard Gerrit Gustafson, prolific Integrity Music songwriter, share about his encounter with Mother Theresa in India. During the course of the conversation he asked what "worship" meant to her. Her response surprised him. She said that when she helped an orphan in the street, when she gave a cup of cold water to a thirsty child, she was worshipping God. After all, didn't Jesus say: "Whatever you did for one of the least of these brothers of Mine, you did for Me"? (Matthew 25:31-40).

As I began to earnestly study this I found more and more evidence that God really does link our worship with our acts of kindness. "Religion that God our Father accepts as pure and faultless is this: to look after orphans and widows in their distress..." (James 1:27a). Amazing! It says nothing about singing or lifting hands. No reference is made to prayer or intercession. Pure religion is looking after those in need.

In the context of bearing one another's burdens, Paul prays that God would "give a spirit of unity... so that with one heart and mouth you may *glorify God...*" (Romans 15:1-6). By bearing the burdens of one another we can come into a degree of unity whereby God is glorified. In this instance, glorifying God, or worship, appears to be a by-product of helping one another in times of need.

I also came across some rather fascinating verses in Psalm 68. "Sing to God, sing praise to His name, extol Him who rides on the clouds — His name is the LORD — and rejoice before Him. A father to the fatherless, a defender of widows, is God in His holy dwelling. God sets the lonely in families, He leads forth the prisoners with singing..." (Psalm 68:4-6). Right in the middle of simply glorifying God, David begins to expound upon God's heart toward those in desperate situations, the heart of a loving heavenly Father who is far more interested in actions than in words.

Worship is more than just singing songs on Sunday morning. Ultimately, it must be even more than singing songs all through the week. Worship must be a way of living. It should encompass all that we do and say, even those little acts of kindness to strangers.

When was the last time you offered a cup of water to someone who was *really* thirsty? Befriended a fatherless child? Participated in a pro-life demonstration? Helped the homeless? Visited a nursing home? Are we really fully worshipping the Lord if our lives are not a demonstration of such things?

One day, during the course of my studying this social justice/worship relationship, I was driving along in my car singing praises to God with a worship tape. I was on a long stretch of highway when I noticed a car with a flat tire. On the opposite side of the road I noticed an older woman walking. I felt a nudge inside to turn around and go pick her up. I resisted, but immediately I remembered that this was an opportunity for a real act of worship. I turned around and took her to a service station. On the way I learned that, although we were each more than 15 miles away from our respective homes, she lived only two houses away from our church. I had the opportunity to introduce myself and invite her to church.

I could have continued on driving, singing my words of worship. Instead I chose to glorify God with my deed, a simple act of kindness to a person in need. That's the real heart of worship.

Often at worship conferences I have heard Hebrews 13:15 shared: "Through Jesus, therefore, let us continually offer to God a sacrifice of praise — the fruit of lips that confess His Name." Frequently this passage is used to help people understand the necessity of giving vocal expressions of praise in every situation. This is indeed a correct under-standing, but if we stop there we miss the context of the passage. The next verse says: "And do not forget to do good and share with others, for with such sacrifices God is pleased." Simply verbalizing our praise and worship to God is not enough — He wants our lives and our actions.

Will *you* accept the challenge? Beyond the Sunday morning singing, let's live lives of worship. Let us model real worship of God for those around us. Let's not be so caught up in the intricacies of music performance that the heart of the Lord is forgotten. He cares greatly about *people*.

Let's take our worship beyond the four walls of the church and offer our lives to the Lord through acts of kindness and social justice to those in need. That's real worship.

Worship:
Spending Time
with God

Definition: Worship is knowing God.

It is time to "consider everything a loss compared to the surpassing greatness of knowing Christ Jesus my Lord" (Philippians 3:8). If the Holy Spirit is speaking anything universally to the church in America it is this: know God. Nothing is more important for us in this hour.

We talk about evangelism and the power of the Holy

Spirit. We talk about the power of taking praise and worship to the nations. We talk about signs and wonders. But it is all just talk unless we know God. Oh sure, we may win a few victories and see a few minor miracles here and there. However, if we will really know God there will be no stopping us!

Someone once said that if we develop a face-to-face relationship with the Lord it will save us from needing to go to a lot of witnessing classes. There is no question that knowing God is the real key to His power. "...the people who do know their God shall be strong, and do exploits" (Daniel 11:32). But even in this there is the tendency to be side-tracked. We want to know Him so that we can have power in our lives. I suppose that this is nobler than no desire to know God at all, and yet it does not seem to be the highest motivation. Perhaps we should consider knowing the Lord regardless of what we can get from the relationship. To know the Lord — I mean really know Him — is what really matters.

I have been thinking a lot about relationships lately. It takes a great deal of effort to make a good relationship. It also takes much time.

As I pondered these things I contemplated my own relationship with God. I wondered if there was anything lacking in the way I related to the Lord. As I did this, I realized there was something in our relationship which could be improved. Let me explain.

There are numerous aspects which make up a solid relationship between two people. There are times of great intimacy. There are times of making requests of one another. But there are also other times where you are just friends — no great lightning bolts out of the sky, no earthshaking excitement, just simply being friends.

Times like this can mean nothing more than sitting together on the porch. At other times it could mean talking about the weather. Sometimes it may mean watching a movie together. Not the stuff of great depth, but still a very important part of building friendships.

We need these times with God, too. I have no trouble worshipping the Lord, and being intimate with Him. By His grace I have reached a level of maturity where the way I feel does not play a major role in whether or not I can worship God. He first loved me, and therefore I will love Him in return. He is worthy, and therefore I will worship.

I also do not have a problem making my petitions known. If I *need* something specific I am not shy about asking for it. If I need guidance, I request it. If I need wisdom in dealing with a particular situation, I will ask the Lord to grant it. Asking God for the things I truly need is usually not difficult.

However, sometimes I do have trouble just being friendly with Him. Please do not judge this next statement until you have read this entire chapter, but sometimes I think I take God too seriously. Certainly, He does not take *me* as seriously as I do. To the Lord I am not a well-traveled teacher and author, or the minister of worship at Christian Outreach Church... I am just Tom. In the same way, there are times that He wants me to see Him not as the Almighty God of all creation, but simply as my friend.

Jesus told us, "...but I have called you *friends*" (John 15:15). Yes, we are to be His servants and worshippers, but He also desires simple times of friendship. He wants to be included in our everyday lives *as a friend*.

While this is true, we also need times that are more disciplined, set apart just for God, to develop and maintain our relationship with Him. This concept is similar to a marriage relationship. Although much time in a marriage is spent together with the children and others, it is still essential for the husband and wife to spend time alone together. The relationship needs those times to become stronger. Likewise, we too need one-on-one time with our Lord.

These intimate moments with Jesus cause us to be more like Him. Perhaps the following poem will help illustrate that point.

> An ancient parable doth say,
> One day a wand'rer found a lump of clay.
> So redolent of sweet perfume,
> Its odor scented all the room.
>
> "What art thou?" was his quick demand.
> "Art thou some gem from Samarcand?
> Or spikenard in this rude disguise,
> Or other costly merchandise?"
>
> "Nay, I am but a lump of clay."

"Then whence this wondrous perfume, say."
"Sir, if the secret I disclose —
I have been dwelling with the rose."

"For we are a fragrance of Christ to God among those who are being saved and among those who are perishing" (2 Corinthians 2:15). If we are indeed to be that fragrance, then we must dwell with Him. We must *know* God.

Even as I write this I can hear the cries of despair, "But you don't understand my situation. Knowing anyone, even the Lord, takes time. And time is something I just don't have!"

I can definitely empathize with this line of thought. From the time I became a Christian I was certain that the Lord had called me into full-time ministry. Yet for twelve years I worked secular jobs waiting for the fulfillment of that which God had spoken to my heart. I never seemed to have enough time to do the things that I said were really important. Deep inside I knew that when I was finally in ministry on a full-time basis things would be different. How wrong I was.

Even today, as I am in the midst of accomplishing the very thing which God has ordained for me to do, I too often find myself putting aside the things which I say are of the greatest value: prayer, Bible study, personal worship, communion with God. All of the things by which I can know God are often pushed aside until a more convenient time.

In this hour we must stop giving lip-service to "priorities" and instead live those priorities. If it means the house is a little messier than you would like it, it is worth it. If it means that you make less money because you work fewer hours, the trade-off is more than adequate.

For a long time I had contemplated taking a personal prayer retreat. Recently I actually went away for two days to seek the Lord. At the end of the time, as I was leaving, I went back inside the cottage where I had been staying to collect my belongings. As I entered the door I felt a tremendous heaviness of heart, and I fell to the floor sobbing. I immediately felt as though I had missed something that God had for me. Then, just as suddenly, I realized that it was not that I had missed something while I was there, but that I had missed something by putting it off for so long.

Now is the time. Regardless of what it takes, this is the key for us in this hour: know God. There is no longer time for life as usual. We must set our course and continue on it steadfastly.

"Therefore, since we are surrounded by such a great cloud of witnesses, let us throw off everything that hinders and the sin that so easily entangles, and let us run with perseverance the race marked out for us. Let us fix our eyes on Jesus, the author and perfecter of our faith..." (Hebrews 12:1).

Knowing God, cultivating our relationship with Him, is worship.

Conclusion

Several years ago I had reached a point where I was pretty sure I knew just about all there was to know about worship. At the time I had been a Christian for 13 years and had been leading worship for nearly 10 years. I taught about worship and worship leading at conferences and seminars across the nation. I was even the managing editor of a leading praise and worship magazine. Although I would not have stated it as such, I really felt I understood the full scope of what worship was all about. How naive I was. "The man who thinks he knows something does not yet know as he ought to know" (1 Corinthians 8:2).

The truth is that at that point I understood only a small portion of what I have written in this book. And today I realize that compared to what there is yet to learn and understand, I honestly know very little about worship.

If you have made it this far in the book, then perhaps your thinking on the subject of worship has been stretched. Maybe you have seen a few things that you had never considered before. If so, then the goal I stated in the introduction, "...that your idea of worship and how it applies to your life will be stretched and expanded to come closer to the fullness of God's desire for you as His child," has been realized.

Please understand that this book only scratches the surface. There is much more yet to learn. Do not allow yourself to get to the point that I had reached several years ago when I was certain I knew all there was to know about worship. Use this book as a springboard to keep learning and keep growing.

I would encourage you to begin to apply one or two (or more) of the concepts mentioned in this book. Don't merely listen to the Word — do what it says (James 1:22). If the Holy Spirit prompted something in your heart as you read — if He showed you something you need to do or change — then be diligent to act upon it.

Above all, keep seeking after the object of our worship, Almighty God. He promises that if we seek Him with all our heart we will surely find Him (Jeremiah 29:13).

Moving a Congregation Ahead in Corporate Praise and Worship

This section is especially for pastors and church leaders. As I travel I am frequently questioned by church leaders about how they can motivate their congregation forward in corporate worship. Their dilemma is that they, as leaders, have begun to see and experience worship beyond a traditional, passive form, and they now desire to allow their congregations the same liberty. Unfortunately, they are not certain how to proceed.

From my experience and observations at churches that have made such a transition, here are some practical steps to making it work. These are four very basic, yet very poignant, steps that will make moving forward in corporate praise and worship a reality.

1. Teach the scriptural basis for worship.

I mentioned in the introduction to this book that people frequently formulate their ideas about worship more from their experience, both their own and others, than from a truly scriptural perspective. Often past recollections mold and shape our thoughts about worship. The things we experienced in church as children, or the style of worship in the church where we first came into a saving relationship with Jesus will too frequently hold more sway in our lives than what the Bible has to say.

Because of this, people need to be taught about worship from a truly biblical perspective. They need to know what worship is, why we worship, how we worship, etc. Many of the concepts in this book are ideally suited for such an endeavor. In teaching these concepts, do not consider anything to be too basic. I am consistently surprised at the lack of understanding of truly scriptural worship.

Additionally, when teaching these principles, do not progress too rapidly. It is easy to get excited about an idea and run roughshod over years of ingrained traditions. Perhaps the traditions need to be altered, but a slower, gentler approach will usually yield better results. The fact is that making a major change in the philosophy of worship may take years for any given church to implement. For us as leaders this may seem like eternity, but for the sake of the people, taking a slower course of action is worth the effort.

2. Teach on grace.

Once you have laid a foundation for worship (by teaching what it is, why we do it, how we do it, etc.) the next step in moving people forward is teaching on grace. People will never fully enter into worshipping God until they understand that He loves them. Many people, even Christians, have a mental picture of the Father as a mean ogre waiting to smack them when they mess up. This image is certainly not conducive to worship.

People need to see that they have indeed been given liberty in Christ. They need to understand that God is *for* them; He is on their side.

When this type of portrait is painted of the Father there is freedom for worship. Love begets love. When we realize how much God loves us, we want to love Him in return. All the teaching about worship we can do will not substitute for a scriptural understanding of the unfailing love of God.

3. Teach on the attributes of God.

After laying the foundation for worship and teaching

about the wondrous grace of God, the next step is to point people to the object of their worship, Almighty God. We need to tell people everything we possibly can about this great God that we worship. They must know about His greatness, His power, His creativity, His holiness, His majesty... all of the things that cause us to be in awe of Him.

When people begin to get a glimpse of what God is really like, they will worship. Just like we discussed in chapter 3 (Worship: Our Response to God), when we behold God our immediate response will be worship. As we begin clearly to articulate what God is really like, the natural response of the people will be a greater desire to worship Him.

4. Ongoing teaching.

The above steps are only a beginning. They must be repeated. It is easy for us to become complacent in our walk with the Lord. Sometimes it is even necessary for us to be reminded of some of the basic aspects of following the Savior. Because of this, ongoing teaching about these things is essential.

It can stir us up to greater fervency to be reminded about the what, why, when and where of worship. We find a freshness in our relationship with God as we hear the simplicity of the grace message. We discover more zeal as we are pointed clearly toward the wondrous God that we worship. Teaching these concepts again and again will yield much fruit in your church.

Appendix B

Scriptural Expressions of Worship

Throughout the Bible there are numerous examples and commands of how we are to express our worship to God. None of the examples listed below are complete in and of themselves, nor are each of them appropriate for every time of worship. They are meant to be an encouragement for us to go beyond our cultural understanding of how we can worship and move into a more Biblical perspective.

Additionally, this is not meant to be an exhaustive list of the physical ways we can express our worship unto our Creator. Even with the opportunity throughout eternity to offer our expressions of worship we will surely never exhaust all of the possibilities of how we can worship God.

Bowing Down — Psalm 95:6 — "Come let us *bow down* in worship..." (see also 2 Chronicles 20:18).
For many this is the ultimate tribute of homage. As we bow in worship we declare that God is ultimately worthy of all that we are and have.

Clapping — Psalm 47:1 — "*Clap your hands*, all you nations."
This can be spontaneous applause or exuberant rhythmic clapping. The Scripture does not specify exactly how to clap (applause, clap in rhythm, clap in rhythm on the off-beat, etc.). It simply tells us to do it.

Dancing — Psalm 149:3 — "Let them praise His name with *dancing*" (see also Psalm 150:4; 2 Samuel 6:14).
Dancing can be reverent, joyful or both. Dancing in worship can be slow and flowing or fast and exuberant. Some have declared this expression as off limits in the Church. Why? It is simply personal preference. We can discuss at great length how we dislike this concept but when we are finished our discussion, God's eternal Word still says: "Let them praise His name with dancing."

Kneeling — Psalm 95:6 — "...let us *kneel* before the LORD our Maker" (see also Daniel 6:10).
Kneeling signifies reverence as one would bow before royalty. We can express reverent worship to God by kneeling before Him.

Leaping — Luke 6:23 — "Rejoice in that day and *leap* for joy..." (see also Acts 3:8).
Leaping is often a spontaneous act of joy. By joyfully leaping before the Lord we can express an emotion in worship which is otherwise difficult to express.

Lifting Hands — Psalm 134:2 — "*Lift up your hands* in the sanctuary and praise the LORD" (see also Psalm 63:4).
Lifting hands is often associated with the act of surrendering. By lifting our hands in worship we are signifying that we surrender everything to God.

Playing Musical Instruments — Psalm 150:3-5 — "Praise Him with the sounding of the *trumpet... harp* and *lyre... tambourine... strings* and *flute... cymbals...*" (see also 1 Chronicles 15:16).
While some believe that only certain instruments are proper for worship, the Bible never confirms this idea. Using a variety of musical instruments can often enhance times of worship.

Shouting — Psalm 66:1 — "*Shout* with joy to God, all the earth!" (see also Psalm 35:27).
In our culture shouting is too often reserved for expressing excitement at sporting events or expressing anger. Shouting can be a very appropriate way to express our praise to God.

Silence — Habakkuk 2:20 — "...the LORD is in His holy temple; let all the earth *be silent* before Him."
Sometimes the best response to the Lord is simple, quiet awe.

Singing — Psalm 147:1 — "How good it is to *sing* praises to our God..." (see also 2 Chronicles 29:30b).
Singing praises to God is nearly always appropriate.

Standing — Nehemiah 9:5 — "*Stand up* and praise the LORD your God..." (see also Exodus 33:10).
Standing is an act of honor as in standing for the entrance of a bride or dignitary. Simply standing before the Lord can be an act of worship.

With an Offering — Psalm 96:8 — "...*bring an offering*, and come into His courts" (see also 1 Chronicles 16:29).
An offering of self, as well as material goods, can be worship to the Lord.

Appendix C

Scriptural Reasons for Worshipping the Lord

S everal years ago someone asked me if I had ever studied in Scripture the reasons *why* are we to praise and worship the Lord. Many of us would probably have difficulty answering that question in the affirmative. We often have some ideas but have never honestly really studied it. In this section are listed a few thought starters, but these are only a beginning point. I would like to challenge you to study on your own the scriptural reasons why we should worship God.

1. Because He is God
For He is our God and we are the people of His pasture, the flock under His care... (Psalm 95:7).

2. Because He commands it
Praise the LORD. Praise the LORD from the heavens, praise Him in the heights above. Praise Him, all His angels, praise Him, all His heavenly hosts. Praise Him, sun and moon, praise Him, all you shining stars (Psalm 148:1-3).

3. Because He is worthy
I call to the LORD, who is worthy of praise, and I am saved from my enemies (Psalm 18:3).

4. For His faithfulness
For the LORD is good and His love endures forever; His faithfulness continues through all generations (Psalm 100:5).

5. For His love
After consulting the people, Jehoshaphat appointed men to sing to the LORD and to praise Him for the splendor of His holiness as they went out at the head of the army, saying: "Give thanks to the LORD, for His love endures forever" (2 Chronicles 20:21).

6. For His greatness
For the LORD is the great God, the great King above all gods (Psalm 95:3).

7. For His salvation
The Lord is my light and my salvation — whom shall I fear? (Psalm 27:1).

8. For His mighty deeds
One generation will commend Your works to another; they will tell of Your mighty acts. They will tell of the power of Your awesome works, and I will proclaim Your great deeds (Psalm 145:4,6).

9. For His holiness
Let them praise Your great and awesome name — He is holy. Exalt the LORD our God and worship at His footstool; He is holy (Psalm 99:3,5).

10. For His creation
You are worthy, our Lord and God, to receive glory and honor and power, for You created all things, and by Your will they were created and have their being (Revelation 4:11).

11. For His power
...We give thanks to You, Lord God Almighty, the One who is and who was, because You have taken Your great power and have begun to reign (Revelation 11:17).

12. For His miracles
When the crowd saw this, they were filled with awe; and they praised God, who had given such authority to men (Matthew 9:8).

OTHER BOOKS BY TOM KRAEUTER

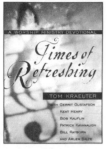

In a devotional format veteran worship leaders draw upon the Living Water and their vast and varied experience to address essential topics, including a biblical view of worship, building relationships, expecting God's presence, and much more! Designed to be read either by individuals or by worship teams, each insightful devotion contains a Scripture passage and teaching from a respected worship leader. A great resource for worship team leaders.

Sale $10.99

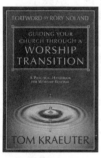

Many churches are considering a change in worship style—or they are in the midst of one. How can congregations walk together through a successful worship transition? Based on solid scriptural principles and the experiences of scores of churches, this wealth of tested solutions and steadfast counsel equips believers with answers that will make a difference.

"This magnificent teaching contains valuable insight...Read and be blessed!"
—Darlene Zschech

Sale $7.99

These two books are so complete and practical they are now being used to train students in Bible colleges across North America. Church music/worship ministries are also using them as study guides to strengthen the ministry of praise and worship in their congregations. In these books you'll find a wealth of information. If you're a beginner or a seasoned veteran, you'll find yourself referring to them again and again.

Sale $7.99

Sale $7.99

Training Resources Order Form

TITLE / DESCRIPTION	PRODUCT #	QTY	PRICE	TOTAL

	Subtotal	
	Shipping/Handling	

US/Canada, add 10% on $0-$50. Over $50, add $5.00 only. For foreign orders
(outside US/Can) add 40% to all orders for air shipment, 15% for surface shipment.

TOTAL

PAYMENT OPTIONS
(check one)

⅃ Enclosed is my check or money order for $_____ in US currency.

⅃ Credit Card
Please bill my: ⅃ **MC**   ⅃ **VISA**   Credit Card Expiration Date:_____

Card# _____

Cardholder's Signature _____

Name____ _____

Address_____

City_____State_____Zip_____Country_____

For Orders:
   Call: 1-(800) 922-2143
   Or Write To:
      Emerald Books, P.O. Box 635
      Lynnwood, Washington 98046